WILDFOWLING TALES

PAST AND PRESENT

Allen Musselwhite

ISBN 978-1-78222-750-2

Photos by the author and Clive Elliston.

Book design, layout and production management by Into Print
www.intoprint.net, +44 (0)1604 832140

CONTENTS

Wildfowling Tales Past and Present

DEDICATION

I would like to dedicate this book to my late father Bill Musselwhite and Uncle Roy Musselwhite for all there knowledge and encouragement they gave to me when I embarked on this wonderful pastime.

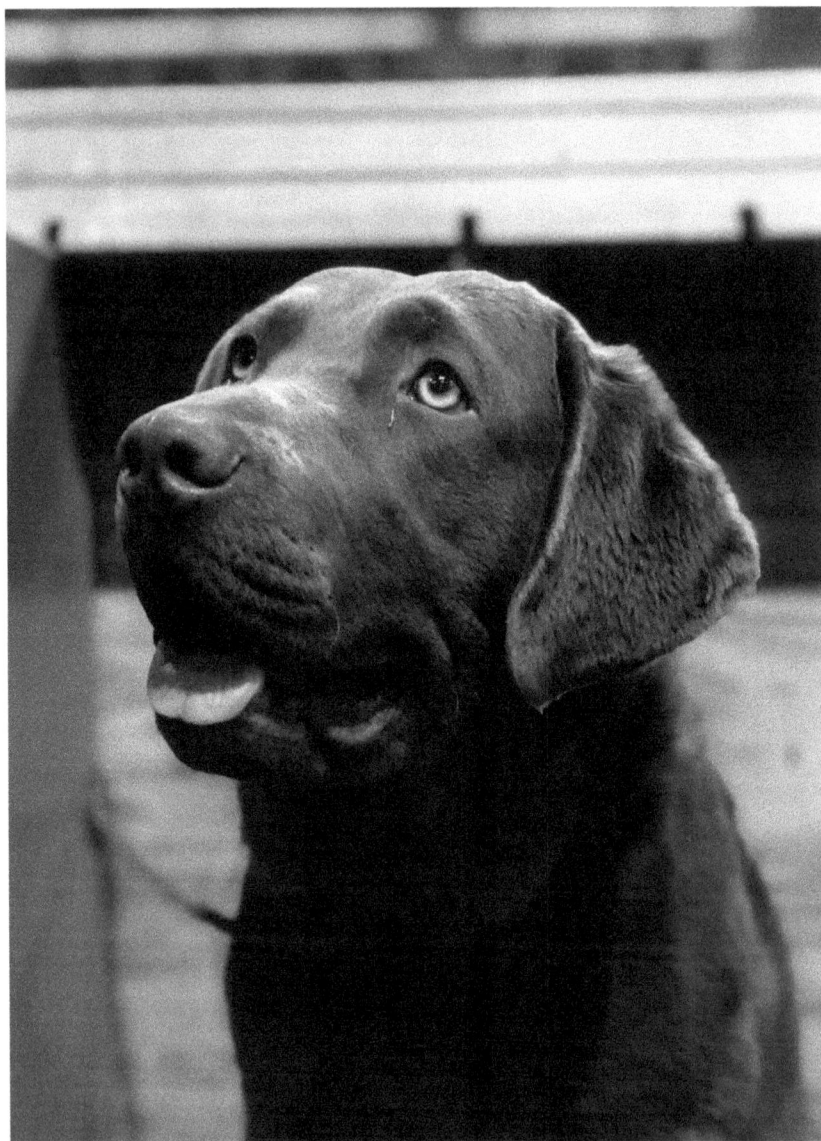

Puntgunner Ebbing Tide "Ty"

INTRODUCTION

I have spent a lifetime wildfowling and involved in shooting and fieldsports. Wildfowling has been in my family for over a hundred years, it's in my blood. I have a passion for punt gunning and have also spent the last year shooting and breeding award winning gun dogs, particularly Chesapeake Bay Retrievers. I decided to write this book as quite often I would find myself relaying some of my wildfowling, punt gunning, shooting and dog breeding stories and advice to friends and people i have met. It dawned on me that I had a wealth of experience and stories that I would like to share with others.

I have put together this book to give you an insight into the world of wildfowling, fieldsports, punt gunning and dog breeding that I have gained over the years. I hope you enjoy this book as much as I have enjoyed putting it all down on paper. I've included some interesting and humorous stories as well from over the years.

AN INTRODUCTION TO WILDFOWLING IN LANGSTONE HARBOUR

In the summer of 1976 I paid my first subscription to Langstone and District Wildfowlers and Conservation Association (LADWACA). I had been shooting with my father and uncles for a few years prior to this, but this was my first real club that I belonged to.

I remember being so eager for the season to start. When the season did start I went out with my father and uncle Roy several times before even firing a shot. I was armed with a Belgium .410 3inch magnum and it soon became apparent that I needed more firepower so my father bought me Bill Ellis's old hammer gun. It was an Armstrong from Newcastle upon Tyne. 12gauge, my first shots with it was a right and a left at Mallard on Hayling Island gravel pit. The seed was now well and truly sown for a lifetime of Wildfowling.

The Club had been formed as LADWACA in 1956, its inaugural meeting was held at the Black dog in Arundel street, Portsmouth. LADWACA was made up of like minded people and families of which two such families are present in the club to this day. Those families are the Atkins family and the Musselwhite family.

The reason for the formation of the Club was to protect the sport of wildfowling, clubs all around the country were being formed at this time. All members of these clubs were also members of WAGBI which stands for Wildfowling Association of Great Britain and Ireland. This affiliation was included in their subscriptions. WAGBI was formed in 1908 by Stanley Duncan and he took the position of Secretary. The first local contact was with a dentist, Dr Kingdon Murrel. There are a few photographs of him in his punt in Langstone Harbour.

Wildfowling has taken place in Langstone harbour for several hundreds of years. Fisherman fowlers used the diverse wealth of seasonal produce available to them, not only for food, but also for income, selling what they caught or shot to local stores, public houses as well as fishmongers and butchers. This practice went on up until just after world war 2.

It can also be noted that there were a lot of houseboats in Langstone Harbour and several at Eastney Lake (which is at the bottom of Locksway road).

It was notorious for fishermen and fowlers to gather at the two public houses called *'The Oyster House Tavern'* and the *'Thatched house'*.

These men would often be seen working on their gunning punts and their fishing boats. One of the Atkins family laid claim to a piece of land that is next to the entrance to the old canal. This piece of land is big enough to have a hut on it, I believe it is called Primrose cottage and I think the date on this is 1903. It is still owned by the Atkins family.

There were several families that worked out of Eastney lake. Some were fishermen, some were wildfowlers and some would be both. There were some oyster beds at Eastney that were owned by the Russell family for a period of time. The oyster spats were put in and left to grow until they were of a size that was harvestable. (more on the Oyster trade later on).

My Grandfather used to work his fishing boat out of Eastney Lake; he was a bit of a rogue. It is believed that during the 2nd world war he used to make trips to the French coast and smuggle brandy and nylons back to England under the darkness of night, for a wealthy businessman. He got caught and served time at his majesty's pleasure.

PUNT GUNNING

It is documented that Punt gunning took place in Langstone harbour as far back as the 1700s, during the 1800s Colonel Peter Hawker visited the area and recorded in his diaries that in his opinion it was one of the finest harbour that he has seen for punt gunning, but had more

active punt gunners than his own harbour at Lymington.

There were several families punting the harbour for generations, the Atkins, Musselwhites, Pycroft's, Bollons and latterly Holdaway's, Sellers also individuals including Lee Freeston & Nick Horten to name but a few.

I believe that there were over a hundred punt gunners at one time in Langstone harbour.

A family from Hayling Island who were very active from the 1800s until the 1980s they were the Pycroft family (who were brick makers and builders by trade). They would punt between the two harbours of Chichester and Langstone depending on the tides and weather conditions.

The Pycroft family made bricks by an old fashioned method called clamps, they would dig the clay locally and fire the bricks on their land. They moved from Milton in Portsmouth to Hayling island as they had exhausted the clay and moved to Hayling Island at the turn of the 20th century.

One of their family members worked in Portsmouth Dockyard and it was said that he made 12 punt guns during his employment at Portsmouth dockyard. I have one of his muzzle loaders and we believe one of his breech loaders.

We know that Sir Peter Scott punted with Harold Pycroft as did Christopher Dalgety, this was during the 1930s up until the outbreak of the second world war. They would punt both harbours.

During the second world war Christopher Dalgety was stationed on Hayling Island and was a frequent visitor to the Pycroft house. Whilst stationed on the island Christopher Dalgety was to train the troops that were to become known as the "cockle shell heroes", a task that nearly drove him to a break down, as told to me by Noel Pycroft.

The Pycroft family had a license to punt the harbours during wartime rationing, with food in short supply this would help the war effort. There is a story documented in other publications that refer to a large number of Brent geese being shot during a six week period, which was vigorously denied by Harold and his brother Albert Pycroft.

The Atkins Family punted out of Milton locks, they were fishermen in the summer and wildfowlers in the winter. There are still some of them to this day, but no punt gunners now.

The last two punt gunners from that family died during the 1990s and after the millennium. Jim Atkins last punted in the 1970s but his brother George punted up until the 1980s. George's son Brian still had George's punt and gun.

In 2010 I restored the punt to its former glory. The gun was in a bad way, but with a lot of work and effort by myself and Lee Freeston we were able to make it presentable and all the action and locks worked, we were also able to remove the breech plug which I don't think had been removed for over 25 years!

The punt and gun are now displayed at shows throughout the south of England.

In 2012 myself and Nick Horten bought Harold Pycroft's old punt that had been built in 1946. We were told of it by a friend who said it was in a boatyard chandlers in Fareham, they had tried to restore it, but not very well. We got the punt back to the barn where we kept the others and work started almost straight away. Within a few weeks she was complete and after a few sea trials she was ready for the coming season.

In 2016 we took the ownership of another punt that was in a very sorry state, it had been made in 1914 and belonged to the late Victor Pycroft, I did wonder if I could honestly do something with it. I think most people would have looked at it and said it was a lost cause, but not me after restoring George Atkins punt I was positive I could do something with it.

I brought it home and onto my driveway, (my wife made a comment about a bonfire) but I could see the potential.

With a lot of work replacing rotten timbers and removing the ironmongery it was starting to look like a punt once more. With the additional help once again from Lee Freeston and Nick Horten, it was nearly there.

LADWACA had another club member called Sean Singleton who had his own boat building business. Sean offered that when it was complete he would sheath it

in fibreglass which he did and now perhaps it will last another hundred years.

MY FIRST PUNT

In 1988 I built my first punt. I was lucky enough to have met a chap from Poole called Sean Adamson who supplied me with some drawings of his punt which was a single at about 18ft. I used his plans but increased the size to 21ft 6, so it was a large single small double. I still have this punt now and still use it. The construction is of ply and fibreglass tape for the joints. All the ribs are inch ply. That punt is now 31 years old and as good today as ever.

I purchased an inch bore punt gun from Lee Freeston, a muzzle loader used for a couple of seasons and sold it to purchase a 1 3/8 Alfred Clayton muzzle loader which I still have to this day.

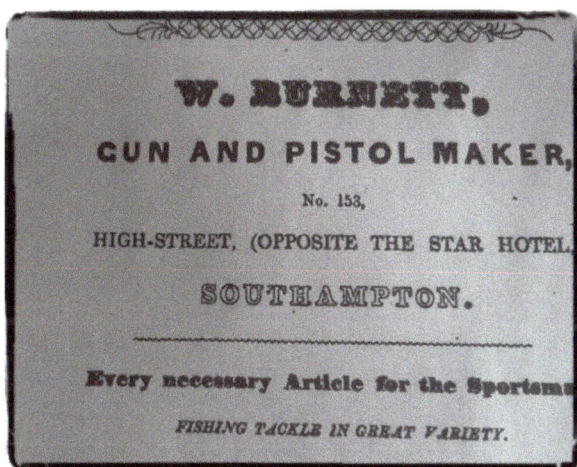

By now I had all the equipment but not enough knowledge to make every trip successful, I called on the assistance of Bert Holdaway. Bert was in his late 70s early 80s by now

and not a lot of patience. On one occasion we were out under the moon. He had rowed the punt all night, done all the setting and all I had to do was make the shot.

I duly took the shot, 8 widgeon on the water, 8oz guns, we got 7 all stone dead. I was elated at our success, but not Bert. *"We should have had all 8"* was his comment.

Bert standards were set very high. I asked him to show me how to scull a punt, he agreed, but it would be the only instruction he would give me. After that I had to practise it until I grasped it, which I assure you took many frustrated hours until I became quite proficient at it, or at least I thought so.

I continued to punt quite vigorously for the next five or six years, notching up a lot of nautical miles and hours.

We were getting fairly good at it and our knowledge that we had gained with the hours spent afloat meant that our success rate was better than it had been before. Our average shot was 16. Things couldn't have been better. Until we had some news that was like a "bomb shell".

Lead was being banned for wildfowling.

What would this mean for punt gunning? We knew it was going to happen eventually, but nevertheless still a shock.

Punt Gunners around the country decided to do some testing with non toxic shot materials, such Bismuth & Tungsten Matrix, the test results proved ITM (tungsten Matrix) was the preferred option ballistically. However, the stumbling block was the price! at the time it was £220 per 7 kilos.

We had no choice, we either paid the price or retired from punt gunning, (which was not an option).

The new shot worked as well as the previous lead shot, it was just a lot more expensive.

I thought I would include the following extract from Colonel Peter Hawker Diaries – see over – because even in the 1800s it was a sought after place to punt, wildfowl or fish as much as it is today. I think it is worth remembering that there have always been restrictions with seasons, although they have changed over the years.

dropped anchor in Langston
harbour about 3, when Singer
(Ward's gunner) & I, lowered a
punt in which we kept survey-
ing the harbour till near 10, at
night. The _shooting_ was _not_ my
object. Singer would ship Ward's
beautiful Stanchion, &, had I
not missed fire (owing to a little
sea that we shipped) I should have
made a grand shot of Curlew-
Jacks. — N.B. Langston harbour
is without exception the finest
gunning place I ever saw; — but, if
possible, more infested with
gunners than Keyhaven.

2nd Got under weigh long before
we were up in order to secure

It would have been expected to adhere to some of them during the 1800s at least. The two restrictions that affected the wildfowling in Langstone Harbour during the Club's existence is the 1954 Protection of Birds Act in which 2 inch guns were outlawed and you could only use 1 3/4 inch as the largest punt gun. Brent geese were removed from the quarry list along with widgeon (which were the stable species for punt gunners).

Then came the 'Wildlife and Countryside Act 1981', where most of the waders were removed, leaving only Waders Snipe, Golden Plover and Woodcock on the quarry list. As with anything that gets removed, it never seems to be reinstated to the list even when recovery is proven.

PUNT GUNS

The punt gun that I used the most in my early punting career was an Alfred Clayton inch and three eighths bore, it is a muzzle loading punt gun.

It was made between 1839 and 1855 whilst he was at the high street Lymington.

A potted history of Alfred Clayton is as follows.

Alfred Clayton was born in 1809. He was married at the age of 35 to Miss Bell Forster who was the eldest daughter of Mr T Forster.

Alfred Clayton gun making business first appears in Lymington in the hand list directory Bailey and Nie, Lymington and Pennington 1843 – 1855.

It is recorded that he was very well thought of by Colonel Peter Hawker and assisted Hawker with all sorts of gun smithing problems.

We know that after the building of Hawker's double gun there were several problems that Clayton resolved for him. Alfred Clayton was very involved with Hawker, he took a patent out for an improved ignition system on a gun that Hawker had designed in December 1850. We know Hawker died in 1853, soon afterwards Clayton moved to 153 High Street Southampton which was formerly William Burnett Gunmakers premises.

William Burnett was at this address from 1843 – 1851 and prior to that William Burnett was at 18 St Marys Square Southampton. Alfred Clayton traded from there until 1871 approximately.

The records state that Alfred Clayton owned a vessel called the Grasshopper which was still registered to him in 1887. This is particularly strange because he died in 1884 in St Marys Road, Southampton. It is recorded that he had a condition which caused softening of the brain. He had suffered from this condition for three and a half years. It's possible this condition could have been as a result of a stroke. He was 75 years old when he died and is buried in Southampton.

There were several Punt-gun makers in the Southampton area. They were situated around the High Street area with Alfred Clayton, William Burnett Patstone and later Patstone and Cox.

With the Portsmouth Dockyard being a source of heavy engineering, there were several punt guns made there. It is said that one of the Pycroft family members built between 10 and 12 punt guns whilst he was employed by the Portsmouth dockyard.

I currently own one, possibly two of these punt guns, the second one I am not sure of its provenance. I have several punt guns in my possession one of which could well be a Alfred Clayton or a William Burnett two inch gun. Unfortunately not marked with any maker's name.

But the likelihood is that it could be from either maker.

In my possession is an engineers gun that is a one inch bore, very crude but usable . Also one and three quarter inch bore by J W Tolley, it is a very heavy gun about one hundred and ninety pounds.

About six years ago myself and Lee Freeston had met an engineer (that I had met in hospital after suffering a heart attack) build a double gun to our design, which he did very well, it is a double one inch bore proofed by the London proof house for eight ounces from each barrel. It is a muzzle loader fired by electronic ignition.

That particular gun is a Musselwhite & Freeston 001.

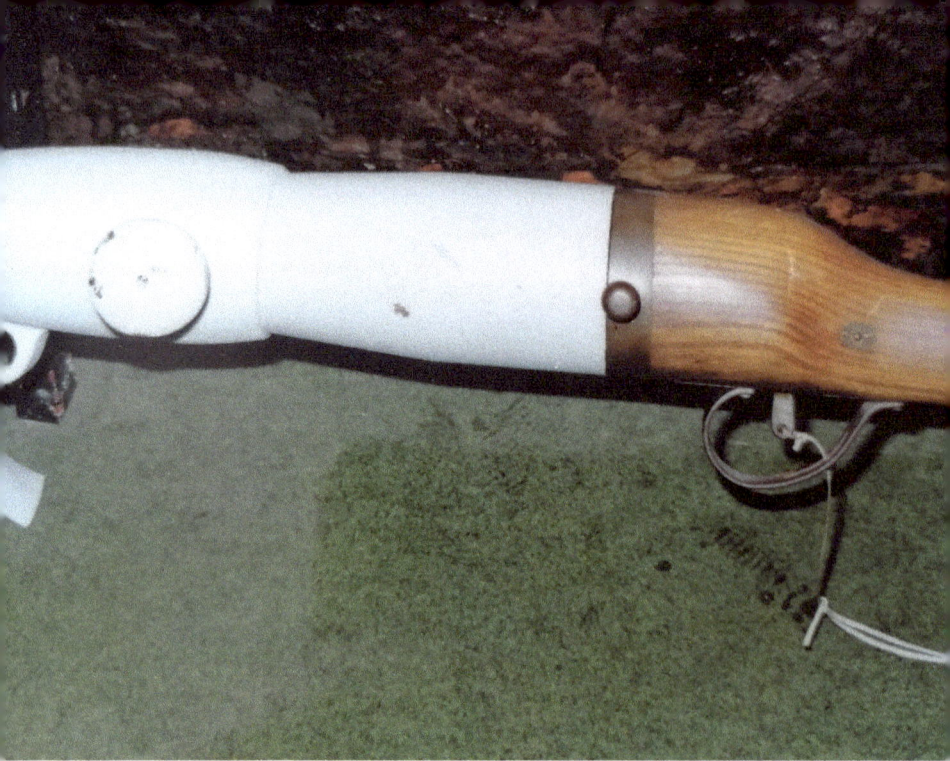

'A picture of Irish Tom so you can see the size of the gun!'

There are several famous punt guns, the biggest being 'Irish Tom' which is held at the BASC headquarters in Marford Mill. It was made for use in Ireland.

This gun started life as a muzzle loader and was bought by Stanley Duncan (who is the founding member of WAGBI —now BASC) in the early twentieth century.

Stanley Duncan converted Irish Tom to a breech loader. The conversion was done by Herbert Coade. This gun was bought by James Robertson Justice, the actor later in the twentieth century.

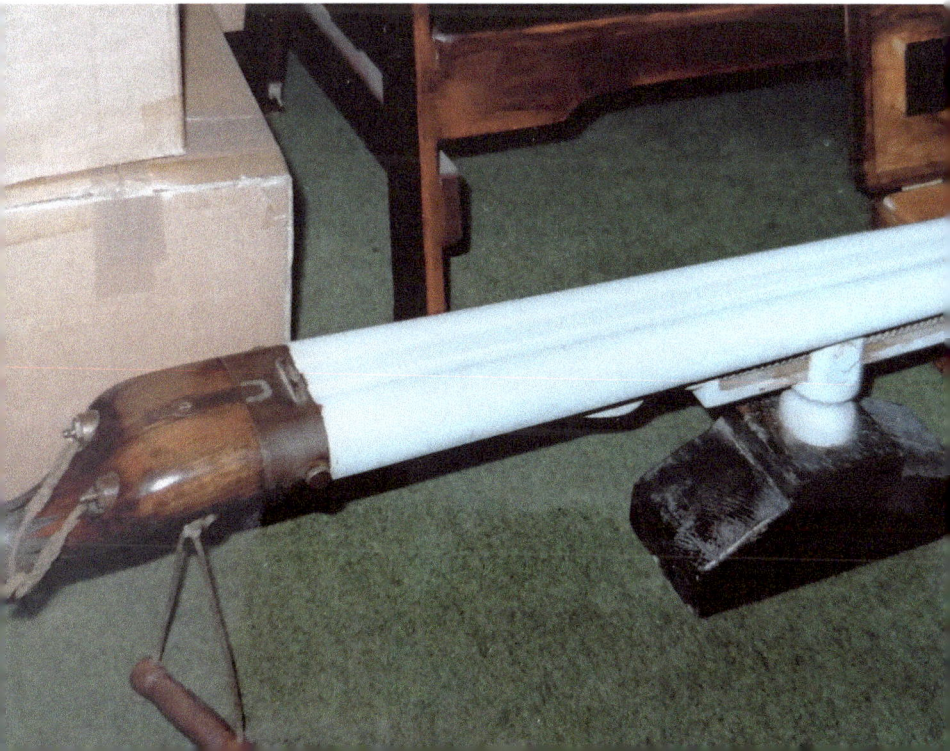

Hawkers double gun is at BASC headquarters alongside another famous gun, a double Holland and Holland. This gun is one of only three ever made. The gun was bought by Stanley Duncan and split to make two single guns. In later years they were bought by James Dorrington and reunited as a double gun again. It now resides at BASC headquarters, Marford Mill. There are many other guns that are known to be of historical importance but these are just a few.

As you can see punt gunning is a big part of my wildfowling career. I am forever trying to find out about the historical provenance of a gun or a punt. Or anything else about it for that matter!

WILDFOWLING IN CHICHESTER

In 1987 I joined Chichester Harbour Wildfowlers Association.

I had not been shooting very much between 1980 and 1987 as like all young men I found the attraction to a lady that became my life. I also found the love of motocross racing which occupied a lot of my spare time, but having a young family took its toll when bones were broken and being a self employed carpenter meant if you were off work injured you didn't get paid.

So my racing career was terminated and I went back to shooting. I had to reapply for my shotgun certificate and the application process had changed a lot and now had a much stricter criteria.

That's when I joined Chichester Harbour Wildfowlers Association, CHWA for short. As a new member I had to do a probationary year with a full member. I was given a contact list of names when I joined. I contacted Clive Elliston from Southampton and we arranged our first foray during October that year, I remember it well. We went to Appledrum at Fishbourne and I shot my first widgeon in a number of years.

I was again bitten by the wildfowling bug.

During this period I was introduced to a mountain of a gentleman called Dave White. Neither of us had met before but he invited Clive and myself for breakfast after the flight.

Clive assured me that this was normal and that there was a likelihood that there might be other wildfowlers there as well. He was right, there were about six of them there with two sittings for breakfast, all washed down with red wine, port & whiskey! I was astounded Id never seen anything like this before. Fortunately at that time I was not much of a drinker, it's strange how that didn't last.

My wife Heather has always blamed Dave's influence over

me and Clive. One of Dave's claims to fame was that he defecated in most parts of the harbour. I remember thinking that I'm not sure I would be telling people that if I was him.

Daves Meals were legendary. We would have breakfast and he would say bring the wife and the kids back for dinner. Clive would bring his wife back as well.

Dinner would always rolled in to tea and the next thing you knew it was 9 o'clock at night.

Dave and his wife Ruth were the most kind and likeable couple you could ever wish to meet. Unfortunately Ruth passed away a few years ago and that left us all with a big void in our lives.

I remember going around Daves for breakfast and I took a friend and fellow wildfowler Pete round there. He wasn't sure that he would be welcome turning up unannounced with me, I assured him it was ok.

Dave welcomed us in. Sit down he said we will have to share this bottle of red. I have only got one bottle but I've got some of the green shit.

Pete looked at me and said, *what's that?* I laughed and replied *you'll find out soon!*

The green shit was a mixture of anything left over from Christmas or holiday gifts, anything that had a little bit left in it would go into the demijohn. It was like rocket fuel.

Anyway, we have a glass of wine with our breakfast and then Dave gets the green shit out.

Well, Pete takes an instant liking to it. He knocks a few glasses back, I could see his eyes start to glaze. I said we had better go as you have work this afternoon Pete and luckily I was driving because Pete could barely stand.

I got him home, he sought of made it through the door, but as you may have guessed he did not make it to work that afternoon. I had to cover his shift because after all I was his manager, I had no choice.

Funny enough he wouldn't go round to Daves again he was always busy when invited.

On another occasion I was out with Dave and Clive moon flighting, very little was happening. I decided to call it a night and went home.

I returned in the morning for the flight as both of them suggested that I had gone home because of an urge that needed to be satisfied. Nothing to do with it, fact is I was absolutely shattered! I think it shows the drink had well and truly taken hold of them that night.

There was a time when the three of us were out and Daves dogs were running around and one of them brought a young signet back unharmed, Dave took it from the dog and released it.

We had walked another two hundred yards and one of the others brought another signet back, Dave duly released that one as well. He decided to put all the dogs on leads as he said this was becoming embarrassing.

I have had many forays with Dave, certainly for my first 20 years in the club. When I first met Dave I asked him how old he was. He said fifty-four the same as my waist size.

We went to a BBQ at Dave and Ruths. We were all sitting in the garden with our wives when one of them said what's that smell? Dave looked up and said, it might be the dog, it's under the patio, perhaps I didn't go deep enough? ... Well, that certainly cast a shadow on the evening, I really didn't fancy anything to eat after that.

I got Dave to join Langstone for a few years in his late wildfowling career. I think he enjoyed himself as by then he had learnt to drive (and that is a loose term!).

Daves driving did not start until he was well into his sixties. He was at best cautious, at worst dangerous. But it did mean he could now get from place to place without relying on other people. I remember on one occasion turning up at his house and his green Suzuki jeep had two big score marks down it, when I asked what had happened he replied, I turned the car over in a lane and a kind farmer used his forklift to turn the car up the right way. I asked if he returned home after the ordeal he said no, I carried on the shoot. I did not realize until after we had spoken he had five dogs in the back the whole time.

I can remember there was an occasion that he had invited me and the wife over for dinner, in the middle of the table was what can only be described as a large saucepan with whole pigeons all around the perimeter in a red cabbage broth.

It looked very uninviting. I did eat some, but it took some concentration to do so.

When Dave first joined Langstone we took him on the Island for the first of September. Dave had bought himself a pair of thigh waders. They looked like surgical stockings on him, I asked if he had tried them on before now he said no as he didn't have anyone to help him. Well we eventually got him in to them, he started to wade across the gutter and got stuck. We knew there was no way that the boots were going to come off whilst we tried to get him across.

After a lot of effort we managed to get him out there. But in our minds we knew we had to get him back in the morning.

Fortunately that wasn't quite so bad, with the aid of a bit of the tide it went quite well. Suffice to say we never tried it again.

Dave played a big part in my life in my early days in CHWA (Chichester Harbour Wildfowlers Association) and outside of the association. I have a lot to thank him for, his knowledge of the area and the knowledge he passed to me.

I have been a member of what was CHWA and short lived title that has now changed to Chichester Wildfowlers Association, for over thirty years.

Things have Changed during that period, some for the better some for the worse, but all in all we are still able to go wildfowling, punt gunning and shooting in general.

We have seen leases renewed, land purchased for shooting. I think we owe a lot to the management committee of the associations that we are members of. In recent years I have become one of the Vice Presidents of the Chichester Wildfowlers Association.

I consider this to be an honour.

There is plenty of shooting available within the association and the club is very proactive always looking for additional shooting for its members.

PUNT GUNNING IN CHICHESTER HARBOUR

On the 14th February a few years ago we set out in the punt myself and Nick Horten.

Not wishing to be late back, (as it was after all Valentines day). We had a hard row against the tide but we knew where there was possibly a good shot.

Being the back end of the season we knew everything would be jumpy.

All of sudden we came across what looked like some Mallard at about two hundred yards away. As always we were able to identify for sure with binoculars. We got down, Nick behind the gun, me pushing the punt. It was a hard stalk as I was pushing against an incoming tide. We got to about one hundred yards and the mallard were starting to get nervous, eighty yards they were still there but twitchy, sixty yards it's now or never.

Nick was just a few more yards, then BOOM!, the gun roared and we went straight into the cripple stopping drill. We only had one to dispatch and we picked up eleven Mallard, a very successful shot. After a coffee, a slow row back with the tide we both knew it had been a very enjoyable morning.

A nice end to a good season.

For over thirty years I have always been out on the thirty first of August with Clive to see the new season in. Which normally involves a lot of alcohol. It's not always the same harbour it can be at least three different harbours but as long as I am physically able to do it I will.

It is much more civilised these days. We don't tend to rough it on the sea wall to sleep.

We now stay in our house-boat (more on that later).

There have been many occasions when we have had a few drinks, something to eat. We would then rest up for the night and get up miles too early for flight. Then struggle to keep my eyes open. You would think that after all these years we would learn. But sadly we don't!

GUNDOGS

This topic always opens up a minefield . Everyone has their own opinion on what's best. It is a personal choice. I have always had spaniels (English Springer) because I liked them, and as I said Big Dave White had them and it was an influence on me.

When I was a youngster and shot with my father we had Labs and later a Springer. After having a very successful springer, I had noticed she did suffer from the cold in extreme weather. I wanted something different from a Springer or a Lab. I saw an advert in the shooting times for a Chesapeake bay retriever for sale. (we looked up on the internet to see what the breed looked like, at first glance it resembled a giant poodle in reality it was nothing like it). I phoned the gentleman up and asked about the dog. He said it was not a dog but a bitch and she was five years old and fully trained. The price was £1250.

I explained that was more than I wished to pay and left at that.

About four weeks later the advert appeared again, I rang the gentleman up and spoke to him again, he said he said his circumstances had changed and the dog needed to be gone by the weekend. I made him an offer which he accepted (the offer was nowhere near the original asking price). I went up on Saturday morning to Essex and collected her. She proved to be the best wildfowling dog that I had ever owned. That set the benchmark that I needed to achieve.

As Fable got older I needed to bring a younger dog on. I bought Fudge, a bitch she soon got called the dark destroyer.

She proved to be a very capable bitch.

Unfortunately I was unable to breed from her due to a prolapsed back end and I had her spayed.

I worked her for quite a few seasons and realised I needed to bring a youngster on, so I bought a puppy from a lady in Warwickshire.

We named our new puppy Fern and again she proved herself to be a very good bitch in the field and on the marsh. I bred a litter from her and kept a bitch back for myself. The bitch was called Flight. She again proved to be very good, but I could not breed from her.

I was now in a dilemma. I was getting to a stage where I needed another dog. Fern had died at an early age and Flight was getting older. I wasn't sure what to do. No litters were due to be born. I was told of an eighteen month old bitch that was available due to a marriage break up. I contacted the gentleman and he told me the lines of the bitch and that she had almost completed her training. I met up with him in South Wales and collected the bitch with the proviso that if I bred her he could have a puppy.

Her name is Zivah. At 2 years old we had a litter from her and I kept a bitch from her called Perdy.

I still work both of them now, although Zivah is getting on a bit now. Two years ago we had a litter from Perdy. She only had three pups, one dog and two bitches.

We decided that after that litter we did not intend to have any more litters.

Ty's Awards

I did keep the dog back to train for myself. His name is Punt Gunner Ebbing Tide TY I'm not one for showing my dogs but I was asked if I wouldn't mind if the sires owner took him to a show. I agreed and didn't think too much more about it.

He won his class! I then entered him for the LKA dog show at the NEC in December 2019. He again won his class and a challenge certificate that automatically enabled him to qualify for Crufts 2020.

I will be using TY for Stud this year (2020). He has had all the health checks completed. So I think and hope that he will produce some nice pups.

If you do intend to breed from any of your dogs the onus is on you to ensure that all the health checks are done prior to breeding. In this Country there is a club called the Chesapeake Bay Retriever Club UK. This club has all the breed information about this particular breed.

I believe that a Chessie is the ultimate wildfowling dog. It will suffer extreme weather conditions because of their double oily coats. They can carry all forms of Wildfowl from the smallest Teal To the biggest of Geese. They are also at home sitting in a pigeon hide. I have used mine picking up, and stood on a peg.

One thing you can say about this breed they are a very versatile Breed (but I am also very biased).

I know a lot or people will favour labs for wildfowling as I've said before it is personal preference. A lab is a lot hardier than a spaniel.

If it is more than one type of shooting that you do then you have to try and get something that is an all rounder. Thats why a lot of people will choose a Spaniel, whether it is a Cocker, a English Springer or any of the other breeds of Spaniel. A friend of mine swears by Golden Retrievers as an all round dog.

He uses them for wildfowling and picking up. There are all sorts of breeds of dogs turning up in the field or on the marsh, one of the most common are Sprockers (a cross between Cocker and Springer).

A Springador is another, which as it suggests is a Labrador cross Springer. I am of the opinion that I want a pedigree dog not a mixed breed.

But that is just my personal opinion and I am sure that some people will disagree with me.

GUNS

A lot of modern day wildfowlers use semi-automatic shotguns these days. All of which need to be restricted to three shots by law, so that it can be held on a shotgun certificate. You can have a bigger magazine for other use. If you have a larger magazine then the gun needs to be held on a firearms certificate. If you are using it for wildfowling then it must not exceed three shots.

One of the reasons that semi-automatics are so popular is their reliability most will rarely let you down. Most of the leading manufacturers produce semi-automatics in their range and in a range of calibers.

I mainly use a three and a half inch chambered 12 gauge semi-automatic made by the Russian manufacturer Baikal, it is a MP153. I have had it for over fifteen years and it has never let me down. I have had to replace one main spring in all that time. I do most of my wildfowling with this gun. It will cycle two and three quarter cartridges right up to

a mighty three and a half cartridge. I also use a three and half inch chambered Browning Gold ten gauge. When out chasing the geese it gives you a little bit more fire power and patterns better with bigger steel shot. It's not for increasing range but putting a better pattern at the quarry you are pursuing. Which you would hope would give you a better chance of killing your quarry cleanly.

The choke I use is an aftermarket choke called a pattern master, and as with all of these aftermarket brands they claim that it will do wonderful things better than the standard factory chokes. I believe it does do a better job than the standard choke (or is that just me thinking it does because I have had some success with it?).

One of the problems with a ten gauge is that cartridges can be expensive. With very few cartridge manufacturers producing them in any quantity, by the end of the season they can be scarce on the gun shop shelves.

Some manufactures produce a 3.5 inch over and under. I have one of these. It is a Lincoln Wildfowler. Mine is finished in the oiled wood finish. It is a thirty two inch

barrelled multi choke. The good thing about being wood finished you can take it on a Game shoot and not feel out of place.

A lot of the three and a half inch over and unders are camo finished. I believe they use a product called cerakote-finish. This finish is extremely weather proof, which for wildfowling is very useful.

Another type of shotgun we should mention is the Pump

action. Very similar to semi-automatic but it is manually operated. It takes some practice to use one and is not the best thing to use at a clay shoot flush. (But it certainly makes your arms ache!) As with the semi-automatic they come in a range of calibers.

Some people still use large bore wildfowling guns. Single and double eight bores and the very exclusive single and double four bores. Some of them are older English guns. Some are modern ones made towards the back end of the twentieth century.

The larger bore guns tend to command a hefty price at auction or on the gun shops shelves. They tend to be very desirable and a reasonably safe investment.

I occasionally use my nine bore. It is a muzzleloader that fires three drams of black powder and one and a quarter ounces of bismuth shot. It was made by J Blanch of London in about 1849. I cant be exact with the year as the Luftwaffe bombed the premises of Blanch during the

second world war and all the records were destroyed.

Sometimes I will take my hammer side by side shotgun

out. It is a T Stenby of Manchester. It was made at about

nineteen hundred.

If wildfowling, I use two and a half inch Bismuth cartridges, loaded with one and one eighth ounces of shot. This is just a few guns that I use. As with any gun you use, make sure the gun is fit for purpose. Before using any gun check that there are no obstructions in the barrels. Remember you would not want to put steel shot through a Damascus barrelled gun steel shot is harder than the Damascus barrels.

AMMUNITION

We all used to use lead cartridges for our wildfowling, ounce and a half of fours for ducks, ounce and seven eighths of ones or BB for geese. We had used these cartridges for years. They worked very well, they were proven, time after time. We had not heard anything about Lead ingestion by wildfowl. I am not sure it has ever been discussed locally. It had certainly not been brought to the attention of clubs management committees. I searched back through all of our clubs archives, and could only find correspondence from the early nineteen nineties. What was interesting is that we took a very proactive view on this matter. In conjunction with BASC we started to test some lead alternatives predominately steel cartridges from America. They seemed to work ok at medium range ducks but not in the same way as lead, certainly not for longer range birds.

We later found out that they exceeded the CIP proof regulations. Testing was halted. We started to test some Eley bismuth cartridges. Again alright at medium range ducks but not that good at the ranges we were used to shooting at.

Another problem with the bismuth was it had a fiber wad not a shot cup. With the testing that we had been doing we were working with BASC and passed the comment on to Eley. They started to produce a bismuth cartridge with a plastic shot cup. Another observation we pointed out to them was shot was quite brittle it needed some antimony added to shot. I was pleased to say they took all of the collective comments on board and produced a viable cartridge .

A couple of our members produced a report that was used by Eley and BASC to promote this alternative. Eleys made bismuth shot available for the home loader. And some large shots available for punt gunners to use as well as the big bores owners.

During this period Punt Gunners were getting increasingly worried. The government at the time had signed up to the African Eurasian WaterBird Agreement. This meant that Lead would be outlawed by the year Two Thousand. So contrary to some peoples beliefs it was not BASC that forced the ban of the use of Lead. They in fact held off the ban for a number of years, to give us a transition period.

It was in fact the government. With this being immanent we had to test the alternatives available to us. Several punt gunners took their guns to Shriverham, a military establishment to test different shot materials.

It was agreed that Tungsten Matrix performed best as this was almost the same density as lead and ballistically similar to lead. This was widely adopted by most punt gunners.

The only problem with these alternatives was the escalated cost. It was in some cases three or four times the cost of lead.

We were able to do some experimenting with different loads and eventually got a good home loaded bismuth cartridge.

The factory loaded cartridges got better as well.

Just when we thought we were ok, Eley increased the price of bismuth shot from thirty three pounds for three kilos to ninety five pounds for three kilos. That made it more expensive than factory loaded ammunition.

I believe there are only three bismuth mines in the world.

We did buy some bismuth ingots and had a go at making our own shot. This worked, the shot wasn't particularly uniform, but it did work. This process was very time consuming and very dirty. This was a very short lived exercise. We needed to find something that was more viable than Bismuth or Tungsten for general wildfowling with a shoulder gun. We revisited steel. There had been quite a bit of research done by home loaders. With use of American powders and some European powders, we could make steel work at a fraction of the price of the other alternatives such as bismuth or tungsten.

There have been other materials such as tin, it really did not work. There is a very good shot called heavy shot, I believe it is a Tungsten iron alloy, very good shot but very expensive. It has very good reports in the shooting press but can be over a pound a shot. There are some other variants of heavy shot but the problem is they are very expensive. I tend to use steel for all my wildfowling these days. With the loading data that is available you can make it work as well as lead, regardless of what some people say. If you think about it, we have removed lead in most other forms where it can contaminate the environment. It was only time before it affected us. I think we must remember even with this legislation we are still able to pursue our chosen sport.

We as wildfowlers are at the forefront of this legislation . That means that we are the experts with these alternatives. We must encourage the use of non toxic shot when pursuing wildfowl .

Whatever the situation is whether it's a game shooting or a small flight pond.

BASC

The British Association of Shooting and Conservation.
The organisation was formed in 1908. It was called
WAGBI then, which stood for the Wildfowlers
Association of Great Britain and Ireland. It was founded
by a man called Stanley Duncan. He owned a gun shop in
Yorkshire. When WAGBI was formed he took the post
of Secretary. As wildfowling clubs were being formed
they would affiliate to this new organisation. This gave
them an unified voice nationally. In 1981 the organisation

changed it name to BASC it was apparent that it was not only catering for wildfowlers but also game shooters and pigeon shooters and most forms of country pursuits.

As time has gone on there are several departments within BASC.

Here is a list of a few :

– Firearms

– Game And Gun dogs

– Deer Management

– Conservation and Land Management

– Wildfowling

– Political Affairs

This is just a few of the departments within the organisation. As members we have access to all these departments if we need them. I think it is worth pointing out that these services are included with our membership. We also get ten million pounds worth of liability

insurance. I have heard it said that other companies can insure us cheaper. That might be the case but what we don't have from other companies is the expert knowledge from the respective departments. If we need to seek specialist advice we would pay for it separately.

BASC has several sub committees I sit on one; it is called the Wildfowl Liaison Committee. Its role is to advise BASC Council of current affairs that are affecting wildfowling, whether localised or nationally. And any recommendations are put before the council. That is basically the role of the Wildfowl Liaison Committee.

Within the wildfowling department there is a publication called the wildfowling permit scheme booklet.

This scheme gives anyone the chance to have a go at wildfowling. Whether you have any experience or not. You will go out accompanied with a guide and hopefully enjoy your experience. The good thing about this scheme it allows to sample this form of shooting at a fraction of the cost of a full membership. In effect you can try before you buy. Another good thing about this permit scheme book is that you can shoot all around our coasts throughout the season sampling all kinds of places. I have known people to book a week off work and shoot four or five different places during their week off.

BASC attends a number of Game fairs throughout the year. We, the Langstone Wildfowlers, attend some of these Game Fairs with BASC. We put on a wildfowling display with the intention of promoting wildfowling to a large audience.

We attend about four or five of these most summers. Any that are in the South Eastern region. That means some times London, Hatfield, the New Forest and Highclere.

We very often attend the autumn show at Ardingly the South of England show-ground In October. This is the last show of the year for us.

Logistically some of these can be a nightmare trying to get four punt guns to a venue. We always seem to manage it. One very annoying question that is always asked at shows, well I don't know if it is asked or stated to me, and that is in times past the old fowlers would fill their guns with nuts and bolts. A fallacy.

If this was to happen the barrel would be rendered useless in a very short time.

Generally speaking we are able to help most people with enquiries about most issues to do with wildfowling. If we are unable to answer a question we will take a contact number to try to find an answer for them. I think as volunteers for BASC we are passionate about our sport and that is the reason for promoting it in conjunction with BASC. It is good to meet people from different parts of the country and sometimes from different parts of the world.

I must mention this, I met a gentleman from America. He asked me about the four punt guns I had on display. I duly told him about each one, he listened and was very interested.

He then proceeded to make me an offer for all four guns. I explained they were not for sale. He offered me a five figure sum, I had to decline his offer even though it was very tempting.

I would urge anyone that takes part in shooting whatever their preferred type of shooting to make sure that you have some form of insurance. Whether it is BASC, CA, NGO or any other organisation.

SHOOTING IN SCOTLAND

During the late 1990s myself and 2 others (Clive and Ian) went to Scotland to shoot in and around the Loch of Strathbeg. It was a very long trip and one that we were all excited about and looking forward to. Clive drove his car with me and Ian as passengers. We were going up there for 3 days shooting. Mainly goose shooting but with the possibility of some Pheasants as well.

We were Staying with a Langstone club member Bob Mccullogh who owned a house in a small village called Newburgh. All 3 of us stayed with him for the duration of the trip. We were to shoot some fields in the morning of the first day, that were close to the flight lines straight from the Loch.

Ian had his dog with us, Sherman a yellow Lab, a very good dog and very capable.

All 3 of us were given instructions to stand in the ditch.

Which was about 5 ft deep with sloppy red mud in the bottom. Decoys were set in front of us. There was a good flight of ducks before the geese moved, but we left them. The geese started to flight about 7.30 am. The flight seemed endless. We all manage to bag some geese. It was very exciting I had not seen anything like this before. We do not get grey geese in the South of England.

That afternoon we went to the Ythan estuary.

We were told that if we went out to the island in the middle of the estuary there was a deep creek to cross. With this in mind I crossed the water to the island, and I was relieved that it was no more than a depression. I continued to the Island, I heard a shout from Clive and Ian I looked up and there was four mallard heading straight towards me. I composed my self put the gun up to them and fired twice.

3 mallard were falling from the sky, I quickly reloaded the trusty 10 bore waiting for the 4th to come back it didn't.

Perhaps that was a bit ambitious.
After picking up the 3 mallard
I returned to the shore and was
greeted by Clive and Ian they both
congratulated me, at this point I
reminded them that my side by
side Gunmark Kestral with a value
of about £100 was indeed equal
to their more expensive guns. Especially Ian's 3" William
Evans that was made for him.

The next morning we headed to the ditch again but
the geese were not playing ball. After an hour or two
we headed further up to some fields. We were able to
intercept the geese and we all managed to get some. Later
that day we headed to Huntley, our intention was to try
and bag a Pheasant or Woodcock. After what seemed to
be hours we reached our destination. It was in fact only
about an hour, it just seemed more. We met up with some
other members of their club. Some of them had dogs.

There was an individual with a springer spaniel, he told us that a few weeks earlier his dog had jumped a barb wired fence and left his genitals behind. We asked if the dog was ok now, he said he should be. I thought that he wasn't really sure. For a man that taught R.E at a local school he swore like a trooper. Which was not what you would expect from a teacher.

The day ended quite well with no adverse injury to dogs or any one. The bag was four pheasants and a woodcock. The last morning, we all had geese from the same area as previous days. The last evening we were all down by the Loch behind some large round straw bales. Ian had said he was not going to shoot instead he would pick up with his dog Sherman.

We had a brilliant flight with geese everywhere, the geese were trying to get to a carrot field next to where we were shooting. We ended the trip with 15 Pinks 3 Mallard 2 Pheasants and a Woodcock.

I almost forgot, and a bag of carrots each.

SHOOTING IN NORFOLK

In 2001 Clive Elliston attended a wildfowling conference in Llandudno, Wales. He met a fellow wildfowler called Colin Wells. Colin is a member of Kings Lynn wildfowlers. After talking for the evening he invited Clive to shoot the Wash. Our friend Big Steve was going to move to Kings Lynn for work. Clive asked Colin if there were vacancies for that season in the Kings Lynn Club. Steve joined the club and Colin became Steve's mentor. Steve also joined Fenland wildfowlers. Clive made contact with Colin during the coming season and we were able to go out on day tickets. We shot Fenland as well as Kings Lynn that season. That was our introduction to shooting the Wash.

We were able to go up for about 3 or 4 days at a time and about once or twice a season. This would be split between Kings Lynn and Fenland. Colin owned a house boat on the Lynn marsh that needed to be replaced. It took him a couple of seasons to get the old one gone and the new one built. It was completed in time for the beginning of the coming season. This would be our first time ever wildfowling from a houseboat. It was a real luxury, instead of sleeping on the marsh we were able to sleep in comfort on a bed and a wood burning fire to keep us warm. There were cooking facilities on the boat, so hot meals, a cooked breakfast, tea and coffee making facilities. What more could we want?

Big Steve was made honorary Chef and was able to produce some very nice meals even though sometimes burning himself. Which I'm sure at times really needed medical attention.

Steve was very good at leaving his cigar in the recess of the door. Colin on many occasions would close the door and crush it, much to Steve's disgust. The boat would sleep 4 comfortably but we have had 6 people at times in the boat, which is far from ideal, but it could be done.

After our evening meal we would have a few beers start

the generator up and watch dvds . Which were mostly wildfowling dvds.

At least one of our meals during our stay would be a Chinese take away, which was only up the road. We could phone the order through and collect it, very civilised.

There is a pub just off the marsh called the Red Cat, sometimes we would go there for a meal and to use the toilets. Believe me, sometimes it was very much needed.

This went on for a number of years. Big Steve eventually bought a third share in another boat that Colin had owned then sold. A lot of time was spent working on this project, by Steve and the other 2 owners. Until they had got it usable.

We were not able to shoot on a Saturday on Lynn because no tickets were issued on a Saturday, and there is no Sunday shooting in Norfolk. So on the weekend we would go back to Steves house.

From there we could shoot Fenland.

The Fenland club has some inland Washes . Sometimes we would shoot some of them. I remember on one occasion we went into the Washes by The Three Pickerels pub and the track was very muddy. Steve got his vehicle stuck up to the axles, Colin was behind us he had seen what had happened. He was able to stop before getting stuck. Steve had boots on and I didn't have any boots on. I took over the driving whilst Clive, Colin & Steve tried to push me out. We eventually got it moving, I was able to get it out, but almost ended up in the river in doing so, catastrophe avoided.

We proceeded with our planned trip.

The walk was about 3 miles. Wearing neoprene chest waders was not the most comfortable walking attire, the water was pouring onto the Washes. Which meant that the depth of water might be a problem by foot.

We did manage to get to our Wash. Clive & Colin in one hide, me & Steve in another. The hides were made from scaffolding that are about 8 foot in height. We set decoys and waited, a few ducks and geese started to move. I shot 3 widgeon and 2 Canadas.

By now we had noticed how much water was coming on. We decided that retreat was our best option, But carrying 2 Canadas off was a mighty task. But I did manage it. I can say that I was very relieved when we got back to the car, we unloaded our gear and went into the pub and had a well deserved pint.

Another occasion we were to take boats on to the Washes. It ended quite disastrous. Steve's boat was quite well equipped but Colin's was not. It took a long time getting to the wash that we had booked. We left Lynn at 8am and we were not ready to start shooting until 1pm due to the time it took us to get the boat and equipment on to the wash.

At about 3pm Colin & Clive's boat overturned, rendering both of them in the water. We quickly rescued them, took them back to the cars and got them home for a hot bath.

We left all the gear there, we just took the guns homes. We returned the next day and retrieved all the gear.

Steve decided to use his outboard on his boat whilst Colin's was loaded on to his trailer. After some tinkering with the engine we got it started, all looked good to retrieve the equipment left on the wash.

Unfortunately this didn't go as well as it could have. We put the engine on the boat Steve & Colin got into the boat started the engine, because it has no gearbox it is direct drive he started it engaged and nearly tipped them both out of the boat, myself and Clive were in fits of laughter. Colin was muttering something about using the engine as an anchor.

That was my last trip to the inland washes and that memory will stay with me forever. I will possibly sometime in the future revisit the washes as Clive is now a full member of Fenland Wildfowlers.

On several occasions we shot Fenland marshes with Steve. Ongar hill was one such place that we shot quite a few times. We were there once when Steves dog called Penn, (a

Flat coat x Lab) found a decomposing grey seal that had

been washed up by the tide. She decided to try to eat it

and when she found it was not to her liking she decided to

roll in it. She stunk really bad.

We also shot at the lighthouse end of the marsh. We could do this on a Sunday as the county boundary was in Lincolnshire and Sunday shooting is allowed in this county. Steve had told us that the predicted tide would allow us to shoot right up until the top of the tide. Alas, surprise surprise, we were starting to get wet with no sign of the tide abating.

I asked Steve if he knew of a way off, he didn't. We will have to stand it out, he remarked. Luckily the tide started to recede and we were able to get off the marsh in relative safety. I think that it reminded me to check the height of the predicted tide for myself rather than rely on someone else and make sure you know the marsh beforehand in safe conditions.

There is another part of the marsh called middle entrance; we were to shoot there this particular morning. Steve was taking a new member out for his final assisted flight. We noticed that there were a lot of geese in the field behind the sea wall, I said to Steve that we were only going out a short distance so that we could stand a chance intercepting the geese as they lifted from the field. Steve said he would continue out to the front of the marsh with his new member, I must point out that this new member didn't have a thumb stick but a curtain pole complete with finial attached to it, all that was missing was the drapes.

Anyway they continued out, the geese lifted straight over us just out of range had we stayed where I wanted to in the first place they would have been well within range, but we all have a degree in hindsight.

Steve and the new member returned to us very wet and minus his curtain pole that had been washed away by the tide when he put it down. This didn't put him off; he rejoined the following year.

We continued to shoot Kings Lynn on a regular basis. We had realised that it would make more sense to join the Kings Lynn club; after all we had been on the list for years but kept deferring it. So we joined, I had been given a key to Colin's boat, he said that I could use it whenever I wanted to. As we were now full members there was nothing to stop us going up to Lynn as and when we wanted to. I took advantage of this on several occasions.

Colin and another chap called John own another boat at the opposite end of the marsh, it was just a hull in fact it was a ship's lifeboat. It is 27 foot long with a 7-foot beam. It is made from steel. They had owned the boat and license for a number of years, but had done very little to it. They asked me if I would like to buy a third share in the boat. Funny how I didn't have to think about it for very long, about 5 seconds.

That was it. I was now a houseboat owner. The only down side was we had to build it.

We agreed a date to start the build. It coincided with my

wife taking our grandchildren on holiday to Majorca. We had a week to get the structure built and to make it watertight.

We were able to get all the materials to the boat with aid of Colin's trailer. Colin and myself had purchased a generator that allowed us to utilise our power tools. Colin and I both have a background in construction that made things a lot easier.

We had agreed what we wanted to spend. As with a lot of situations not all can agree. Colin and myself decided we would spend what was needed to make it as best as we could.

After 3 days the structure was built it was watertight. This was done at the beginning of September. Over the remainder of the season we were able to complete it and on the last day of the season we slept in our boat for the first time.

The boat has evolved over the last few years. We have 12V

electrics which are leisure batteries charged by solar panels. We have 240V electrics and the supply is a generator. It also has a wood burning fire, fully insulated in the walls and it has a gas cooker. We even have a flat screen TV, not that we use it that much. A comment that was made by a committee member it's not a council house, I think this is a bit of jealousy.

We have all the creature comforts should we need them.

A couple of years ago Colin & John sold their shares to Clive. We now split all expenses 50/50.

Myself and my wife use the boat in the summer months to take the grandchildren up there for a weekend break, we insist on no TV, no phones, just time spent enjoying the surroundings.

During the season I go up to the boat every month from September till February, normally 4 days at a time. More often than not I come back with a duck or some geese.

I was able to finish this last season with a right and left at

Pink Footed geese. I was truly elated.

The club has just renewed its lease for another 5 years which should secure us for the near future with the houseboats.

PLACES OF INTEREST IN LANGSTONE HARBOUR

Langstone harbour and its surrounding coastline has a number of WW2 structures from pill boxes to anti tank blocks. There is a structure on one of the Islands known as a decoy town. Its main purpose was to detract the Luftwaffe from bombing Portsmouth Dockyard.

Leslie Marsh was a builder from Emsworth and His company was placed on Admiralty list for defence contracts.

He was awarded this contract and duly built it, the structure is still there to this day. I believe that it is one of only two remaining in the country.

I understand that there is a preservation order assigned to it. Also, there is the remains of a Mulberry harbour that broke its back whilst being towed out of the harbour.

All around the harbour there are at least 4 pill boxes that remain intact.

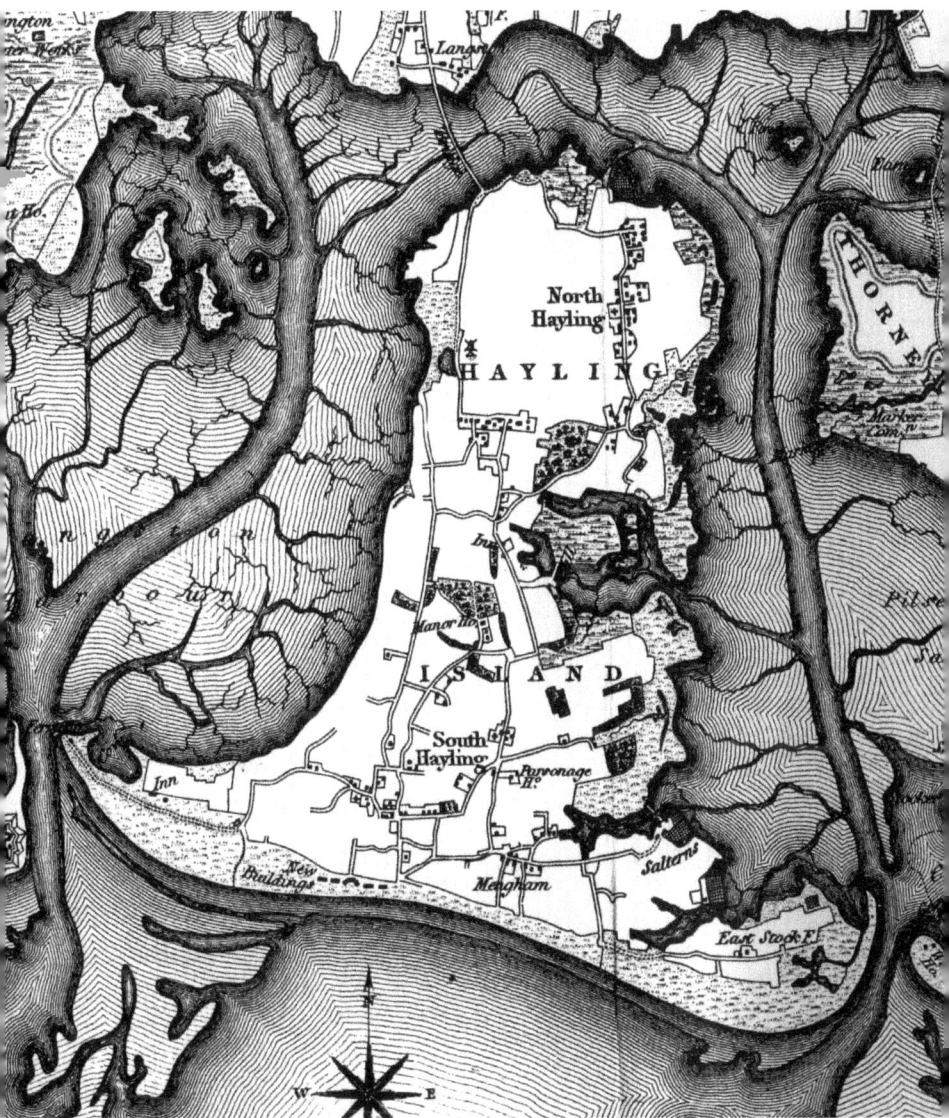

THE RUSSELL FAMILY OYSTER HOUSE

Langstone harbour was a renowned oyster harbour with several companies and families plying their trade in the harbour. This is the history of one such family and is taken from an article that I wrote and is published in Portsmouth Records Office.

The old Oyster House, Farlington Marsh (now demolished)

MATHEW RUSSELL
1776 – 1846

Mathew Russell was born in 1776 in Portsea in the county of Southampton as it was called then. When he was a young man he made his living as a pilot in Portsea ferrying Naval personnel to and from their ships. There is no information that I can find about his childhood. Mathew married on the 12th November 1798 to a spinster called Jane Tilley at St Marys church Portsea. Jane was born in the same year as Mathew 1776 in Portsea. During their marriage they had 6 sons and 2 daughters. I can only find reference to 5 children in later years unless 2 of them died at an early age.

In 1815 Mathew and his young family bought a small Islet on the south eastern point of Farlington marshes in Portsea. This is when he started his business with his eldest son David and became an oyster merchant in Langstone Harbour.

Local historians believed that he had rented this tiny Islet, but he had in fact bought the freehold to this piece of land. By 1819 he had a house built on the Island, there was also a house built on Farlington marshes, whether this was one of their homes as well remains a mystery. The construction of the house was very basic. Four rooms, four fireplaces, one in each room. exterior walls covered in tar to protect the building from the elements. In the 1841 census Mathew Russell (Elder) gave this as his address he called it New Milton. He had 18 acres of mud flats where they grew oysters. This included what was known as Crastick creek. Mathew later called it Russells lake, and it still called Russells lake to this day. The Russell

family had oyster leases around the harbour. This included Eastney Lake, it was leased from John Burrill (esq). In 1839 Mathew took up temporary residence at Bennetts hill doctors, then later Cherbourg France.

In his absence his wife and son continued to run his business.

It is possible at the time of his absence he could have spent his days locating stock for his oyster business.

During the 1830s Mathew Russell was implicated by other Oyster merchants for trying to have a monopoly on the oyster fishing in Langstone harbour. It was said that he was using illegal underhand practices to out produce his rivals. He refuted these accusations, and what I have been able to find out is that no action was taken by the fishery board.

On the 11th December 1846 Mathew Russell died. His funeral was at St James Church Milton and he was buried in the graveyard there. His last Will and testament Listed that there were only five benefactors to his will.

As I said earlier unless 2 of his children died at an early age or he may have just not included them in his will.
I think the latter is most likely. (you will see why later).
He left all his freehold house and land to his Eldest son David with whom he started the business and his other four named Children in the will were to receive an annuity annually.

The will is very complex and is written in 19th century legal terms, it makes for very hard reading.

As you can see there seems to only be a few pictures or paintings that exist of this marvellous house that was used by a very successful local business

JANE RUSSELL
1776 – UNKNOWN

Jane Russell married Mathew Russell in 1798 in St Marys church Portsea. There is very little known about Jane other than it is documented that she survived her husband and continued to receive an annuity annually after his death.

She was the same age as him.

At this time, I am unable to confirm the date of her death, but I believe she is also buried In St James Cemetery Milton in the 1841 census, her address is documented as New Milton fishery Farlington.

DAVID RUSSELL
1811 – 1875

With the death of his Father David Russell took control
of the family business which thrived under his leadership.

David and his family took up residence at the Oyster
grounds, where I think there were two dwellings one
on the island and one on Farlington marshes itself. The
reason for this thinking, there is the remains of a dwelling
on the south east corner of the Farlington marshes
landward side, but also in the 1851 census it lists David
Russell and his family of six at the oyster house New
Milton and another family at the same address Called
Charles Fleet and a family of five.

So, I think that there were in fact two houses, not one.
David had 3 sons and 3 daughters. David Emery, Andrew,
& James. Martha, Anna & Alice.

All the sons and grandsons worked for the family business,
which was making serious amounts of money.

David died on 28th September 1875. He left a fortune to the sum of £7000 which was divided between his six children.

The daughters with larger cash sums than the sons, but the sons had inherited the oyster business, which was continuing to thrive.

Some of this family's cousins were continuing to farm oysters at Eastney lake, but the primary business was still at New Milton. David was also buried at St James Church Milton.

The above picture is the old Oyster House which was also known as the Black house due to the tar that was used to weatherproof it.

MATHEW RUSSELL JNR UNKNOWN DATES

Mathew Russell, I believe might have been the son of Mathew Russell (senior). He is listed as living in Southwick West Sussex as an oyster merchant. In 1851 he took a lease on some mudflats at post creek (now known as ports creek) and the marshes. For the sum of £6.00 per year for a period of 12years.

There is not much known about this gentleman other than the lease was taken out in 1851.

The other interesting fact if he is the son of Mathew Russell snr this lease and his involvement in the oyster business took place after Mathew snr had died.

HENRY RUSSELL
1856 – 1916

He returned in 1899 and bought the winkle market in Langstone High Street. From there he continued to trade in shellfish. He had 3 sons Augustus, Horace & Percy. Henry also had 2 daughters Ethel & Adelaide. All his children were born in the county of Kent. On his return to the area he also purchased Langstone house, in Langstone High Street which was right next door to the Winkle Market. Henry traded from the winkle market buying all forms of shellfish from locals. Some of which were professional and some that were semi-professional adding additional income for their families.

The family still had an interest in the oyster house and was still occupied during the early 1900s.

On the 22nd of April 1913 the house, the land of 18 acres was put up for auction in London auction house as a freehold purchase.

Since the death of the Dean of Winchester in 1902 due to the consumption of contaminated oysters, from Emsworth. The market for oysters from that part of the country had dried up. It is believed that the property did not sell.

The house and some oyster penns remained for a long time, after the house was unoccupied on a regular basis. Henry died in 1916. His 3 sons continued with his shellfish business up until the early 1950s.

The winkle market building was bought by Lt Col Selwyn Guise Cutler in 1954 and turned into a house. Both Langstone house and winkle market are still there to this day (2017).

The picture shows the remains of the old oyster house. You can see the foundations of the old house.

AUGUSTUS RUSSELL
1885 – UNKNOWN

Augustus Russell was the second eldest son of Henry Russell. Like his father and ancestors, he was an oyster merchant. Augustus was also an active punt gunner as well as an oyster merchant. I know this to be true because I have his elevating gear on one of my punts.

I have also heard stories of travelling punt gunners using the old oyster house to overnight in, when punting Langstone and Chichester Harbour. Gus as he was commonly known was involved with the Royal Navy. He was on a patrol boat protecting inshore waters of Langstone and Chichester Harbour during WW1. The Commander of his patrol boat was John Buckle of Farlington Portsea.

ETHEL LONGCROFT (NEE RUSSELL) 1884 – 1967

Ethel Russell was the youngest daughter of Henry Russell. At the age of 42 she married a Gentleman called Charles Longcroft. He was from a well-known family of solicitors, from Havant. They married in St Nicholas church Langstone High street. The church had not been allowed to carry out wedding ceremonies, so they had to get a special license to be married in that church.

Charles bought Langstone Manor House during the 1930s for their marital home. The grounds of the house had two other houses built for his staff. Prior to this he lived at Langstone mill house.

Ethel died in 1967 and Charles in 1974 she was the last surviving relative from the Russell dynasty they are buried in Warblington Cemetery.

Oyster island and its land is now owned by 3 individual people all with a common goal of protecting it from eroding any further.

YOUR AUTHOR

As the Author of this book I tried to relay some humorous tales which are all true, and some factual information on subjects that I hope you find interesting. I felt the need to share some of this information with you before it gets lost in the passage of time.

I hope you enjoy this book.

Allen Musselwhite

OYSTER HOUSE CHAPTER

I have spent many years researching and collating the information that makes up this final chapter about the mythical house that used to once reside in Langstone harbour.

Over the years it has become a passion for me to share details about the history of a very overlooked important landmark in Langstone Harbour.

To this day the foundations of this house can still be seen when the tide is out, and many have spoken of a rumour about an 'old black house' that used to reside in Langstone Harbour. My own interest was sparked, and investigations began. It seemed there was very little known about the origins of this building. If you have any information about the 'Old Oyster House' or would like to contribute to future documents then please send an email to

Allen.Musselwhite@sky.com

www.ingramcontent.com/pod-product-compliance
Lightning Source LLC
LaVergne TN
LVHW070013090426
835508LV00048B/3379